Onyeka Nwelue was born in 1988.

He is an Academic Visitor at the African Studies Centre, University of Oxford and a Visiting Scholar at the Centre of African Studies in the University of Cambridge.

He has published over 20 books, including the award-winning novel, *The Strangers of Braamfontein*, which won Best Indie Novel at 2021 Crime Lovers Award and the 2021 ANA Prose Prize.

He is the founder of the Oxford-based James Currey Society.

A BANQUET
for PIGS *and*
VULTURES

A BANQUET for PIGS and VULTURES

A Play

By

ONYEKA NWELUE

FABULA/Plays
an imprint of
Abibiman Publishing

New York & London

First published in 2023 by Fabula/Plays,
an imprint of Abibiman Publishing

© Onyeka Nwelue 2023

ISBN: 978-1-7392767-1-3

The moral right of the playwright has been asserted.

for my father,
Sir Chukwuemeka Samuel Nwelue,
who died the week I finished writing this play.

CHARACTERS

Ogbuokiri – *an alcoholic carpenter who makes coffins.*
Sam – *an oja player who goes around barefoot, playing for people in exchange for food.*
Akunne – *cousin of Professor Nwokeke and the leader of Umuokpu*
Uduma – *the husband of Akunne – a lazy thief.*
Obianuju – *the wife of Professor Nwokeke*
Ebuka – *only son of Professor Nwokeke*
Nneoma – *only daughter of Professor Nwokeke*
Udenta – *Professor Nwokeke's womanising, prodigal and only brother.*
Chief Ezekwe – *rival of Professor Nwokeke*
Miss T – *a deranged young woman who loves to dress up in colourful clothes with her face painted.*
Chemist – *a quack pharmacist who treats both humans and animals with Paracetamol.*
Madam Ndukwe – *a primary school teacher who loves to interact with all these people in her house, while preparing food for them.*
3 police officers – *Officer Kunle, Officer Edet and Officer Lucy.*

Cast

Prof Nwokeke – Ekweozor Phrank
Woman 1/ Nneoma – Presh Talker Nwankwo
Woman 2 – Gongo Ammanawaji
Woman 3 – Amanda David

Ogbuokiri – Enuma Charles
Paul Bearer – Odiwe Azubuike
Chemist – Uzoechi Ikenna
Priest – Afam Chukwudi
Ebuka – Tochukwu Victor

Extras
Padre Stanley
Amaechi Bobby

FOREWORD

If there is ever a play written in the heat of the moment to rail at an obnoxious socio-cultural practice that has emerged and has become the staple in the African society, then *A Banquet for Pigs and Vultures* by Onyeka Nwelue is one of such. The rites of passage that attend deaths of all kinds in the African world have their specific protocols that are culturally determined and are guided by reasonable philosophical ethos. Nowadays, indigenous values have been eroded and deep-rooted cultural practices have given way to the barrage of modernity and deceptive religious proclamations. The ever present poverty and hunger have joined up with the anomies of the African world and all have been brought to bear on the way we bury our dead, which has led to the prevalent pseudo-culture of lavish, materialistic and gut-driven funeral ceremonies for all manner of dead persons.

The author and playwright in this largely ghostly or gothic monologue of a play attempts to express justifiable outrage at the overwrought gastronomic and materialistic concerns of African funerals that have devalued our concept of life , living and the threnodic relationship between the world of the living and the dead. Who is in the best position to define the hypocrisy, subterfuge and vanity that surround any funeral obsequies or ceremony other than the dead itself? The playwright answers this by making use of a ghost character, uncannily not listed as a character in the play (Prof Nwokeke) as the narrator of the funereal drama of the play. The satiric jabs that logically follow the allegorical title of the play (A *Banquet for Pigs and Vultures*) comes from the mouth of the dead man, a know-it-all man in life and a see-it-all entity in death, as he looks on detachedly at the events and happenstances attending his own funeral.

The play itself in its conception and style fits smugly within the postmodernist artistic practice of the author in which a form can transmute and metamorphose into another wherein poetry flows into prose and drama binds both. The language is declamatory and imbued with the irritable urgency of stemming the debauched pseudo-cultural practice that is the subject of the play. The play as it is can exist perfectly as a literary dramatic text to join up other such texts in the African literary world that dwell on the drama that dogs the transition from the land of the living to that of the dead. On stage, where a play is often completed as drama or theatre, I foresee this text calling up already a form in the hands of a dexterous director and a resourceful actor, which is monodrama. Onyeka Nwelue, in *A Banquet for Pigs and Vultures,* has contributed a new text to engage an old disturbing subject in a new way and to a still largely experimental avant-garde dramatic form.

Denja Abdullahi
Playwright, Poet & Theatre Director
Former President, Association of Nigerian Authors (ANA)

ACT I

Enter PROFESSOR, dandy, grey-haired, pompous, stout, and dressed in white. He paces about the stage, angrily, muttering curses. To one end of the stage is a set up of chairs on which are seated a group of women; they are the Umuokpu, a prestigious and powerful clan group made up of the family's first daughters. They quarrel over their shares of tea and bread, the sharing of which is presided over by AKUNNE, quarrelsome woman.

PROFESSOR NWOKEKE

(addressing the audience)

I thought they had left their husbands' houses to come and mourn me. Just look at how they batter displeasure and greed over food. Imagine the unabashed gluttony! One would think they have never eaten for days.

(Moves closer to Akunne)

I wish I could hammer some sense into that head of yours. It was you who swore never to set foot in my house since I wouldn't buy Keke for your husband. That slacker and thief! Yet you forgot that he squandered away the Two Hundred Thousand Naira I provided him to start a small business with. Foolish me! And to imagine that I gave him that money just after he was sacked from the palm oil mill for theft. I only encouraged his frivolity. For a man arrested for smuggling a drum of palm oil out of the factory, I should have let him rot in jail. But I spent money in settlements, to secure his release. What did I know? The fool that I was.

(Pointing at Akunne.)

Yet you opened your mouth to call me a stingy man! Me, Professor Nwokeke! A stingy man?! Was I being stingy when I took responsibility for your only child's education up until university? But that boy was cut from the same cloth as your husband. How was I to know? He chose cultism over academics, and it was his waterloo. If only I had put all that wasted resources to better use!

(Hisses and turns to another woman in the group)

And you! You peddled rumours targeted at my person, that I got my money from some diabolic means. The kind of stories you people concoct when your idle minds go on their flights of fancy! You would never read nor engage in wholesome entertainment. How could it have been that you went about telling people that I killed my son so as to renew my source of wealth? How on earth were you able to arrive at such far-fetched, nonsensical, fabrication? And how did you come to believe it enough as to repeat it to another? Now look at you. You have been here all night, instructing my children on the type of food and drinks they will serve Umuokpu in the house of a ritualist. Tufiakwa! People of my generation have no shame.

(A woman enters, walks over to the Umuokpu and addressed Akunne.)

WOMAN
The rice is almost done, but the meat they are to present us with is not befitting of our status. I have told them that if they bring out that meat here, there will be trouble.

UMUOKPU WOMEN
What nonsense! Yes, there will be trouble!!! These people don't have respect!!! They don't know and respect tradition!!! We will teach them!!!

PROFESSOR NWOKEKE
Just take a look at them. One would think they are doing me any service in leaving their house to come feed in my house since last night. Oh, yes! They have been here all night, doing nothing but eat, drink, constitute noise and make demands. And since morning none has returned to their husband's houses. Last night's ash remains cold in their hearths. Consider for once that they are yet to finish eating tea and bread and they are already spoiling for rice and meat. What sort of humans are these? Did they truly come to grieve for me? Or is this an excuse to escape the monotony of their meaningless lives? I see nobody grieving.

AKUNNE
Nneoma!!! Nneoma!!!

(Nneoma hurries over to the stage.)

What is this I am hearing about the low quantity of meat you people are getting ready for us?

Did we tell you that we are dogs? Did we leave our husbands' houses to be insulted? We will rather leave with dignity than allow ourselves be insulted.

NNEOMA

(kneels down)

Please, accept my apologies. I am truly sorry. I never knew that this was the situation. Don't be angry. I will look into the matter immediately. Please, don't leave.

UMUOKPU

You better do!!! And do that fast!!! Be quick about it!!! It is almost past breakfast time!!! Are you waiting for the food to get cold before you serve it to us?

PROFESSOR NWOKEKE

(He moves to Nneoma and attempts but fails to lift her from where she is kneeling and pleading with the Umuokpu.)

Why are you pleading with them to stay, eh? These people are of no use other than to consume resources and occupy space. How has humanity benefited from their existence? But here they are, eating and becoming a burden. This is not some eating contest, for Goodness' sake. What difference will it make to anybody whether they stay or leave? Allow them to leave. After all, they will not contribute anything at the end of the day.

(Nneoma leaves. Shortly afterwards, one of the cooks hurries in with a mini cooler full of beef and places it in front of Umuokpu as their faces light up with joy.)

PROFESSOR NWOKEKE

(He commands the cook.)

Will you come take back the meat? Didn't you notice I was telling Nneoma to ask these women to leave my house? And you went ahead to bring meat.

(Gesturing at the cook)

Look at the person I'm speaking to. She's walking away, as though I am making no sense. This is awful!

(Hurries over to the cook and makes to tap her.)

Are you hard of hearing? I'm speaking to you and you are walking out on me.

(The cook doesn't feel anything, so he moves to the table where the meat was dropped and tries to lift it, but to no avail. Akunne calls one of the Umuokpu to share the meat. He tries to obstruct the woman from taking the meat, but she carries it and begins sharing as ordered.)

I know where to catch you people at the end of today. I will make sure you don't get those two he-goats and yams you customarily take home at the end of the funeral party. Gluttons!

(He storms away from the scene.)

ACT II

The Anglican priest with his assistant are seen alone with the artistically-crafted and well-detailed coffin for the religious Anglican preparation and reconciliation rite(s). Other attendees are expected to join the Priest and the dying person for the rest of the funeral activities. There is music at the background playing appropriate selections as the congregation arrive and gather.

Ogbuokiri staggers in, the first to arrive the funeral scene to ascertain the final positioning of the coffin in its right place.

PROFESSOR NWOKEKE

(facing the audience)

While on my hospital bed, I had critically pondered over what existence would mean for me afterwards. I imagined paradise, angels and loved ones who have gone before me. I imagined a euphoric piazza. I conjectured the gorgeousness of heaven to be a great place of bliss at a time of grief, offering hope that life after death is not just a wish but a promise fulfilled. I am a Professor, an erudite one for that matter. I have sat, wined and dined with the crème de la crème in the psychiatry domain. I started out with very sound academic achievements from elementary school, proceeded to Ezeoke community grammar school and finally bagged a medical degree from the prestigious University of Nigeria, Nsukka. Nigeria was fair then. The federal government awarded me a full scholarship for my post graduate studies where I specialized in psychiatry.

I was one of the pioneers of the Psychiatry department at the University of Nigeria Teaching Hospital. I rose through the ranks and became the registrar for two consecutive tenures. I religiously served the University Teaching Hospital before I moved finally to set up my own private healthcare company. Life was decent for me. I am not affluent, but I am contented. I am not a religious person, but I ensure to be kind, empathetic and philanthropic when it is inevitable. So many people say I am uncouth, rugged, stiff-necked, arrogant, proud and all sorts of innuendos. But they have failed to see my core values of hard work, consistency, persistence, excellence and integrity. Begin with small things, that you may achieve great is one strong proverb I keep dearly. *(Attendees are seen coming in as the funeral service begins.)*

PROFESSOR NWOKEKE

(Standing to one side of the stage observing everything. Ogbuokiri causes a scene as he staggers while trying to reach out to one of the chairs.)

While in my bed, in my most assailable points I called my wife and children and warned them not to throw a carnival funeral for me. Obviously they had only pretended to respect my wishes. What a disappointment. Now just look at this frivolous, naughty, loose-guarded, uncultured Ogbuokiri. He never honoured me. Never! Not even pretentiously. He puts it on my face whenever we have a brush.

(Looking at the finely-crafted coffin made by Ogbuokiri)

Ogbuokiri made this coffin. I made it known, on my sick bed, that Ogbuokiri should make my coffin. Although he has something against erudition yet I value the beauty which he seeks with his craftsmanship. One would even say that he achieves sublime arts with his carpentry. This is the only thing that endears him to me. Other than this he is a colossal disgrace. A black sheep amongst his kinsmen. Degenerate drunk. He renders very poor customer service to his clients, even the esteemed ones amongst them. More than once I had referred him to my friends, and each time he had made a mess of things. Are you aware that Ogbuokiri was born to an important Ezeoke family? He schooled here, in this village and would nearly have finished secondary school. But he didn't. He was a ruffian, played truant, bullied fellow students and was always getting into trouble. I think he went as far as the senior secondary classes because of his success in athletics. But then he wouldn't sit for his final exams. Everyone persuaded him. They told him that he would be given an opportunity with a ministry in the federal government, but would Ogbuokiri agree? No. He is a stubborn person - this one! He said it is furniture making or nothing. Ogbuokiri has since then made an appreciable fortune for himself. But between the two of us, it has mostly been quarrels.

(Ogbuokiri falters on his seat, and would have fallen but gets a hold of himself.)

PROFESSOR NWOKEKE

(Clears throat)

I summoned Ogbuokiri one day when I needed to get doors fixed for my new house. He did all the necessary surveys, gave his quotation but wasn't happy that I presented contract papers for him to sign. He didn't sign the papers then. He said he distrusted paperwork, and because we were both kinsmen, I shouldn't be making him sign papers as though he were some stranger. But then he returned two days later to sign them. I think the promise of money was too much to ignore, especially when he thought of his mounting debt at the bar. We signed the papers. The job was meant to be completed in two months. But two months passed and allo Ogbuokiri could come up with were excuses as to why the job was incomplete. You know how these artisans behave.

(He walks to the front of the stage)

Dissatisfied with everything I paid a visit to Ogbuokiri's workshop. To my utter surprise, he had not even gotten the materials together for my job. I was mad. If you were in my shoes you would have called the police too. Of course, that was what I did; call the police. It was the only option other than gouging out his bloodshot eyes.

At the station Ogbuokiri showed no remorse. He behaved so lifeless like nothing was happening. I admired his strength though. But it was too extreme. I just had to let him go. He finally completed my job and it came out excellent so much that I forgot the trouble he had put me through. I had no regrets that I had commissioned Ogbuokiri for the job. The doors in my house looked as though imported from Italy.

(Gesticulating with his hands)

He paid attention to the minutest details. Ahhh! Ogbuokiri, the man blessed and cursed at the same time.

Are you also aware that Ogbuokiri is a glutton? Can't you see that he has looked forward to my funeral when he would have so much to eat and drink for free? Isn't he seeing it as his ultimate victory over all the criticism he had received from me all these years? I had referred Ogbuokiri to Barrister Chime, my best friend. Chime is an Oxford-trained lawyer and has worked for a handful of top global law firms. Because Chime had nothing but praises for my doors on one of his visits and coincidentally needed a skillful carpenter for his house, I sent for Ogbuokiri. The moment Ogbuokiri arrived, I began to regret my decision. He smelled like a brewery even though he didn't exactly appear drunk. And because he appeared to have control over his faculties, Chime thought it wise to put aside his displeasing appearance and get on with the business for which Ogbuokiri had been summoned. I respected Ogbuokiri that day. The suggestions he came up with! Ingenious. Chime was pleased and I was assured within me that Ogbuokiri would deliver an excellent job. They both settled for prices and terms of payment. Chime made him sign contract papers and then paid him a deposit. The stipulated time for this job was longer by two months than mine. Ogbuokiri never commenced the job when he was supposed to. For three days I called at his place but he was nowhere to be found. God knows, I was worried that Ogbuokiri would default on the terms of agreement. This concern made me restless and unable to eat. Chime on his part was already furious with me. But I assured him that everything was in order. Eventually I was able to get a hold of Ogbuokiri three days later. And after much heated exchange of words and threats, Ogbuokiri commenced work on the project. He didn't finish at the stipulated time, as you will expect. But he did a most satisfactory job when everything was completed. Chai! Ogbuokiri has indeed dealt with me.

(Clears throat)

Why would I forget this one event? Mbanu! This particular threatened to destroy everything. Did you know Ogbuokiri impregnated one of my nieces from my maternal side? Yes, he did. He even went as far as trying to get her to run away with him to a far-away place. I was smarter. It happened that Ogbuokiri met her while carrying out my building project and they fell in love with each other. They had seen each other a couple of times. Even though I suspected them I did not think my niece's sense of youthful wantonness knew no boundaries. Imagine such a promising teenager planning to elope with Ogbuokiri. I was later to find out that Ogbuokiri had told her lies? Yes? Such wicked and mischievous lies as you could ever imagine. Firstly, he lied to her about owning a large piece of land in a highbrow area in Owerre and even went on to show her pictures of his former clients' mansions, claiming they were his. During that time, I observed Ogbuokiri. He suddenly became a dab version of his usual self. It was the pregnancy that revealed everything, and, furious as I had ever been, I arranged for him to be beaten. Yes, I was that furious, especially that Ogbuokiri had wrought his mischief right under my nose. And so I behaved as every others whose conduct in such circumstances I often looked down on. I had Ogbuokiri beaten up. My friend, a Colonel in the Army, saw to it. After then, I planned to have Ogbuokiri rot in a police cell where he would never prey on adventurous teenage girls anymore. But first I sent my niece back to her parents. She has the baby now. A boy, so sweet, innocent and promising to bear no semblance in attribute or form of the rascal who sired him. And as though to always remind me of the fact that I made a mess of my duty as a guardian, they made me the boy's God-father. I forgave my niece. But Ogbuokiri has harboured an unspoken hatred for me ever since.

ACT III

The opening hymn is sung as attendees are seen entering in pairs. SAM is playing his oja, praising the ones amongst the guests who look influential.

PROFESSOR NWOKEKE

They have come together to mock me. Yes? Mock me! If not mockery, then what is all this for? Every one of them here did not agree with my ideologies. They cringed at my philosophies and ridiculed my core values. They are not *woke*, as millennials will put it. I tried in so many ways to keep them abreast with latest happenings around the state, Nigeria, and the world as a whole, but it all turned against me. Poor people! Ingrates par excellence! Instead, they come here deceiving themselves like the men of Umunna in Cheluchi's *The Son of the House* – the men of Umunna only showed up to eat and issue commands about which choice parts of slaughtered goat were to be given them.

(The Anglican priest is joined by the attendees for opening prayers.)

PROFESSOR NWOKEKE

(looks seriously as the Anglican priest performs the other funeral traditions.)

The Anglican Church has been dear to my heart. Always has been. I was a most devout parishioner in my diocese. I sent my contributions towards any ongoing church projects. The cathedral of the new diocese that was recently created in Ezeoke was single-handedly renovated by me and my family. The Anglicans believe that when a person dies, the Holy Spirit is released from the body to be returned to God while the body is returned to the earth that had sustained it through life. I have been dead for three days now and I haven't experienced such. Is this where life all ends?

(SAM stops playing the oja as the funeral service is in its very sacred stage. The Anglican priest directs hymns and prayers as attendees stand to take them)

PROFESSOR NWOKEKE

(Stares angrily at the pretentious attentiveness of the attendees as the Anglican Priest goes on with the funeral rituals. The attendees rise and take the second hymn in harmony while some are seen crying reminiscing on the lyrics of the hymn. Sam plays a soft oja sound to follow the rhythm and tempo of the hymn.)

Sam! Stop playing that! I need to think!

(turns to the audience)

You see, Sam and I were like cat and rat. I have known Sam for a very long time. Though, a fantastic *oja* player and a skillful instrumentalist in his own right. He has very bad attitude towards his personal development and he is not a good listener. Just like the old saying goes "He who speaks a lot learns little".

One time, I had an opportunity to nominate a creative artiste in instrumentation for an all-expense paid trip to the Netherlands for a 2 year workshop to hone their creativity and make their skill marketable. As a youth developer and philanthropist from Ezeoke I would not want to have that pass my people since it was a once in a life time opportunity. I reached out to Sam. Sam had this deep-seated hatred for me of which I was not aware of. I wondered how people manage such hatred when they don't know you too well. They just rely on hearsay and never take time to know the truth about what they hear. I will not blame Sam, though, he is small-minded. The selection was getting close and a number of important documents had to be put in place for the smooth onboarding to this creative boot-camp in the Netherlands. Sam had no passport and he never made any effort to get one even with the amount of money he makes. He has never for once taken any musical classes. He is a village champion. Prides himself as the best *oja* player. I pitied him whenever I came across him at a number of functions I attended with friends in Ezeoke. His sound was traditional and stale. No innovation. His dexterity is zero. His greatest achievements were to play for December returnees from Lagos and abroad, village festivals and he never tried to ply his trade in major South eastern cities to gain more recognition and exposure, and improve upon the quality of his life. That was how Sam missed that opportunity. I was pained. That week when other participants boarded that flight I laid curses on him and my inside of hearts bled for my people. What names did I not call him? A popular saying goes thus "All men have three ears, one on the left of his head, one on the right and one in his heart". But I can tell you that Sam has none. Just take a look at him!

(He regards Sam with contempt.)

ACT IV

While the service is in progress, Professor Nwokeke notices, to one side of the stage, the pallbearers in a happy mood. Each one has a bottle of beer in his hand which they sip. Besides them is a crate and a litter of empty bottles.

PROFESSOR NWOKEKE

(He looks at them disdainfully.)

You believe you have a profession, don't you? You left the comforts of your homes to play with Professor Nwokeke's body. I don't blame you at all. I would blame my wife and children for engaging your services. My wife is aware of how much I dislike this type of service. I frowned and halted the pallbearers who used my late father's lifeless body to do jonjoloko, a blatant mockery of a respected Chief like him during his funeral party. See the loafers here today, drinking and get ready to make a play thing of my body. Like I said, I don't exactly blame them. I know whom to blame.

But come to think of it, what is the essence of pallbearers making showbiz with the dead? Why would people, in the name of showing off during burial funerals, allow these young men to play with the dead, especially a person who has in all ramifications distinguished himself when he was alive? Is there any caricature more than playing and making money with a great man's lifeless body? Is there anything more demeaning to the person's stature than that?

PALL BEARER 1

(excitedly)

I wish more people like this will die. This is a big man's burial. The pay is really good and there is so much to eat and drink. We have to do our job very well today so that people will see how good we are, and when another big man dies, they will call us. Imagine how much they have sprayed us this morning from the morgue to the church.

(brings out a wad of cash and counts)

Seventy thousand naira!

PROFESSOR NWOKEKE

(aggressively.)

May the vultures skin you alive! Your father and the members of your family will die every day! Has poverty and avarice altered your sense of reasoning so that you now pray for people to die? Thank your Chi that I didn't bring my AR-15 rifle with me. I would have blown off your skull.

(He scans the Seventy Thousand Naira.)

PROFESSOR NWOKEKE

From the morgue to here, see the amount of money they have raised from making a show of my lifeless body. Some of the people who sprayed this money haven't paid their children's school fees or eaten good food at their homes. They sprayed money to show off that they belong with those doing well in society. None of those who sprayed this money bought apples, paw-paw, or cucumbers for me when I was sick in the hospital. They prefer to spray it on my dead body! That's the height of the wickedness of man. Men spend their own money more on the dead than on the living. Chukwu aju!

(He looks at the crates of alcoholic drinks consumed by the undertakers and counts the bottles.)

One! Two! Three! Four! Imagine the bottles of beer these people are guzzling. In this state, I can't begin to imagine what drunken show they would make of me after the funeral service. Professor Nwokeke, you have really suffered. Something must be done. I need to speak to the Eze-In-Council about these pallbearers. To the best of my knowledge, this is not the way pallbearers behave. There is a need to show them the burial funerals of military men and how they conduct everything with dignity and respect. This negative impression of dancing with the dead in order to make money must stop.

Exit.

ACT V

Sam finally finds a place to sit in the church as the priest delivers a sermon.

PROFESSOR NWOKEKE
Better that you have your seat

(pointing at Sam)

Sam is a mess of himself. I am sure he is full of regrets. Sam had another encounter that would change his life but this time I guess 'his village people' were primarily instrumental to this one. Sam had an opera kind of concert gig courtesy The Music Society of Nigeria (MUSON) at Lagos. The information got to him through one of his very close acquaintances who worked at this prestigious Music organization in Lagos. The week of his departure he was faced with a ghastly accident while returning from a function in Enugu. He was in a coma for two months. The accident resulted to a fracture around his neck which needed a total of three surgeries to correct. He survived it. He couldn't make it to the event in the long run. This accident changed his life till this moment.

(Three uniformed police officers enter; OFFICER KUNLE, OFFICER EDET and OFFICER LUCY. They stand guard around the fringes of the congregation with watchful eyes.)

PROFESSOR NWOKEKE

(Smiles as the Police officers arrive the scene. He moves close to them one by one and whispers to their ears while simultaneously pointing his fingers to suspicious attendees.)

You see them! Yes, those ones (*pointing his hands frustratingly*). They are not here to mourn or pay any respects. They only came for sight-seeing, eating and drinking. They came to see how the Anglican priest dressed up for my funeral. Just see how they are observing the quality of the chairs to know if it was better than the one of Late Lt. Oko Emeka's family used for his funeral. The quality of guests that came to pay tributes too is one of their parameters to assess the quality of the funeral put up for me.

Numb-skulled, dunder-headed, meat-headed, dip-stuck and bone-headed set of humans. They have come to reap where they have not sown. They have come to give fake eulogies about someone they chronically despised. Indeed a Prophet is never recognized in his hometown.

(The Anglican Priest encourages an act of faith and then leads the congregation in prayers for the dead. The litany is said as the people responds in harmony with a repeated sentence i.e. have mercy upon us)

PRIEST
Lord have mercy upon us

CONGREGATION
Lord, have mercy upon us
Christ, have mercy upon us
Lord, have mercy upon us.

PROFESSOR NWOKEKE
What mercy are they hoping to receive? I cannot just fathom it. God will not have mercy on you.

(The Anglican priest leads the Commendation and Farewell. The priest stands and a period of silence leads into the prayer of commendation.

The deceased is entrusted to the love and mercy of God. Ogbuokiri points fingers to the coffin direction and his mouth moves with a smiling face as though he has won a lottery)

What does Ogbuokiri thinks he is saying?

OGBUOKIRI

(aside)

I dislike educated people and Prof is top of the list. Prof never supports my ideas. He always calls me a failure. When he was alive he never said anything good about me.

(PROFESSOR NWOKEKE shuts him up as though OGBUOKIRI hears him)

(The pallbearers lift the coffin as the Anglican Priest follows and then the attendees. They stop at the graveside. The committal is sung. The Anglican priest leads the prayer. The second hymn is recited. The body is lowered to so much wailing. The Grace is finally said.)

See where I finally end up

(looking as his body is lowered to the grave).

This life is indeed short. You will come here with nothing and definitely leave here with nothing.

(He turns to face his wife.)

I thought you claimed you loved me with all your heart, and that you couldn't live without me, yet you stand there watching them lower me here without taking any steps to follow me.

(hisses and shakes his head)

The lies we tell ourselves.

(Miss T enters.)

Everyone calls her Miss T. It was a name that had stuck on people's tongue for so long that they had forgotten that the T stood for Theresa. She had always maintained a trim figure from when she was a young girl in college. She was reputed to tend to her beauty with the right cosmetics that were in vogue. It was said that among her peers she was one of the most desirable and even though her vanity gave her father concerns, yet her mother prided in the knowledge that her daughter was beyond the reach of the young men in Ezeoke and that one day she would get some rich suitor who would have no problems being as generous with his money as Theresa's beauty deserved.

Suitors came as everyone expected, from Orlu, Akokwa, Oguta. The young men in Ezeoke gulped their silent jealousy as worthy men came from afar off to win a dangling fruit in their backyard, but then there would be an extravagant wedding to look forward to and so they all drew comfort in this.

Everything changed one day when Miss T returned home one day, very much unlike herself. Her friends who brought her in said that they had gone to a party in Mbammiri and while sailing in a boat across the sea, she had begun to act strangely.

Miss T never became herself again and with time everyone accepted her state to be an aspect of the village life. She would walk around murmuring to herself and grinning at things unseen. Sometimes she acknowledged when being spoken to and at other times she didn't. Despite her mental condition, she was always to be seen dressed in colourful gowns, with her face extravagantly painted.

(Caterers take up a corner of the stage and begin to lay tables. Some young men set chairs in a row.)

PROFESSOR NWOKEKE

This is fraudulent! Pure fraud! Where did they get the money to put up these wastes? I see.

(still shaking his head angrily)

Is it not with my hard-earned money? Ofe nsala! Ofe Onugbu! Jollof rice! Fried rice! Bread fruit! Abacha! Barbequed chicken! No! No! No! Is this what I get?

(The mourners begin to head towards the row of chairs. MISS T approaches the front row laughing hysterically while other attendees look at her with such disdain. CHEMIST is seated quietly observing the whole event. MADAM NDUKWE comes exactly after the funeral service proper is over. She moves from one chair to another exchanging pleasantries with the attendees and then heads straight for the caterer's table to make a choice of food from the buffet.)

PROFESSOR NWOKEKE

Whoever drinks on credit gets drunk more quickly? The tongue of the fool is always long. Indeed, to ask a favor from a miser is like trying to make a hole in water.

I never thought while I was alive to see this mundane and depraved set of people attend my funeral.

ACT VI

While the Highlife music entertainers and caterers are busy entertaining the guests, CHIEF EZEKWE strides in with his AK-47 rifle and fires three rounds into the air. Some of the guests who are out of his sight almost abandon their food to take flight but remain when they hear the lead singer of the Highlife music entertainers eulogising him.

PROFESSOR NWOKEKE

(With an expression of displeasure.)

What is this unrepentant arch-nemesis here for? He must be overjoyed to have witnessed my demise. He also fired three rounds from his AK-47 rifle into the air to express his joy at finally seeing this day - a day he had yearned for.

(He rushes aggressively closer to Ezekwe, who is spraying wads of crisp 1,000 naira notes to the Highlife music entertainers eulogising him while one of his *escorts clutched his AK-47 rifle and a black briefcase stuffed with money.)*

PROFESSOR NWOKEKE
You have been labelled persona non grata here, Ezekwe! Get out of here now.

(Looking around for the police officers.)

Officers! Please, come promptly and bundle this bête noire out of this place.

(He notices that the police officers are not coming as instructed. He moves to shove Ezekwe out, but he just stands there showering the wads of cash and smiling. He veers away and turns to the Highlife music entertainers.)

Will you stop your exaggerations of what you mistake to be this man's virtues? I thought you were hired to entertain the guests and not just one man who walked in from nowhere. You focused all of your attention on him, as if this were a personal show or something. You people must refund the money you received from my children.

(It appears that the Highlife entertainers ignored his threats and proceeded to praise Chief Ezekwe.)

PROFESSOR NWOKEKE

(Shakes his head regretfully)

Is this how death has turned Professor Nwokeke Magnus, a fierce fighter, powerless? Causing my adversaries to spit in my face? Is this why they say that when a lion gets lame, an antelope would come to get retribution? But, death, why?

Ezekwe used to be my bosom friend until the incident that occurred in 1984. When I met Obianuju, my dear wife, I didn't know that Ezekwe had already proposed to her, but she declined his marriage proposal. Obianuju was like Sidi in Wole Soyinka's The Lion and Jewel Play, while I and Ezekwe were like Lakunle and Baroka. The only difference from the play was that Obianuju accepted my marriage proposal, who is regarded as Lakunle, and turned down Ezekwe, the Baroka. Yes, it is true that Obianuja was the dream of every man in Ezeoke, but if I had known that Ezekwe had proposed to her, I wouldn't have taken a step, let alone proposed to her to be my wife. Maybe that's how Chiukwu wanted it. It was the day I told Ezekwe that the Akwaugo, as we fondly called her then, had accepted to marry me that he raged in anger and accused me of snatching his wife, despite all my efforts for me to sort out things with him, they were proven abortive, and from that day, he saw me as an arch enemy and competed in everything in Ezeoke with me. He would always say that I won him by snatching his wife, but he would never allow me to win anything again. It was because of me that he left Ezeoke for the city of Ontisha, and after a period of two years, he came back to Ezeoke extremely rich, with no one knowing the source of his wealth. Some rumours had it that he used his manhood for money rituals though I didn't pay attention to those kinds of stories. My main concern was how he came back to attack me on almost everything.

I remember the time the Ezeoke community wanted to confer me with a Chieftaincy title for my philanthropic and humanitarian gestures, especially attracting a European non-profit charity organisation to establish a world-class health centre in Ezeoke that has attended the health needs of the people in Ezeoke and other neighbouring communities. Ezekwe went to the Eze of the council and wanted to bribe him not to confer me with the title. However, the Eze of the council rejected the enticing sum he offered them. For that, I salute the Eze in the council of Ezeoke! I ga-adi, Eze! Still, Ezekwe didn't relent. He has challenged me almost everywhere, even in the harvest and bazaar in the church. I defeated him in all. But death has made me a loser today! Death, you are a hex!

(He spots UDUMA bending down as if he wanted to scratch his ankle, only for him to pick up some money on the ground and stuffs it inside his shoe without anyone noticing.)

PROFESSOR NWOKEKE

(shouts at UDUMA.)

Onye ohi! UDUMA, onye ohi! Your cup has gotten full today.

(Strides over to Uduma and makes to grab him, but can't.)

So, you are a thief indeed. I remember Akunne sobbing in the police custody that you were innocent when you were arrested for theft in the palm oil mill. So, if she had sworn in the name of AMADIOHA to prove your innocence, she would have joined her ancestors by now. You will not escape this today. Officer Kunle!

(He moves to call Officer Kunle.)

ACT VII

(The funeral party is at its climax; every guest is fully entertained. Professor Nwokeke goes about to get a general overview of what is happening. He notices some groups of guests laughing out loud while listening to Ogbuokiri, who is drunk and babbling.)

Ogbuokiri

(aside)

Onye oke-amamihe alana! I thought he was immortal. Nwokeke, if you say you are a strong man, come out and fight me.

(One of the guests cut in to remind him that he forgot to add the title 'PROFESSOR' in the name.)

Taa!!! gbafuo there! *Prof* or *Professor* gbakwa oku!

PROFESSOR NWOKEKE

(Regards Ogbuokiri with regret.)

Even the Bible says clearly in Proverb 20:1 in the Good News Translation that drinking too much makes one loud and foolish. What else should I say about Ogbuokiri? If children are only gifts from God, I would rather remain childless than have a child like Ogbuokiri.

(Hisses and moves out of the place. He notices CHEMIST talking at the top of his voice to a few of the guest seated next to him.)

CHEMIST

That is what exactly killed him ... elephantiasis of frontal lobe of the pituitary rotundata. It happens when a patient of Professor Nwokeke's calibre doesn't periodically carry out prognosis to check the state of his pulmonary and arterial urmm .... urmm ... this is a syndrome, you know. You will have to get a basic knowledge of physiology and anatomy to be able to understand where I am driving at.

PROFESSOR NWOKEKE

Quack! Take a look at how you're deceiving yourself and messing with the brains of fellow idiots. Continue to fill their bellies with rubbish. I bet your days are numbered for all the atrocities you have committed in Ezeoke, especially the incorrect medical prescriptions and abortions you have performed on underage girls, which have taken many lives.

(He notices Madam Ndukwe stash foods and drinks into her bags.)

PROFESSOR NWOKEKE

(Irritatingly)

Why do people act so rapaciously even at funeral gatherings? Why is this woman hoarding foods? Since she arrived here today, I haven't seen her spend a dime to support my family. And I definitely know that if food, drinks, and gifts were removed from funerals, people like her would not come.

(Suddenly, Miss T is seen arguing with the caterers.)

PROFESSOR NWOKEKE
Mad people would always showcase themselves in public.

(turns to the caterers, exchanging words with Miss T.)

I don't know why you are wasting your energy on an insane woman like Miss T. Don't you see the way she is dressed? Everybody in Ezeoke knows she is mad, though there are many mad people in our community who don't know they are, and have refused to submit themselves for psychiatric evaluation and possible psychiatric help.

(The caterer doesn't hear him and continues to engage in verbal combat with Miss T. Even as Officer Lucy comes to that point to calm things to no avail.)

I can see that you have the strength to talk. Ngwanu continue. He who fights the insane is also insane! Ndi ara!

(He hears the oja playing and turns to see Sam eulogising Chief Ezekwe seated with an air of importance. Anyone who is sensitive would notice that Sam's eulogy for Chief Ezekwe is laden with praises on some glorious conquest. Sam knows there has been some long-standing animosity between Chief Ezekwe and

Professor Nwokeke, therefore he is subtly applauding Chief Ezekwe for defeating the professor.)

PROFESSOR NWOKEKE

(shakes his head in disappointment)

Death is indeed terrible! Not everyone who attends a funeral party is there to mourn. Some of those who didn't come to mourn are the enemies of the dead who came to gloat and glory in his death. Sam and Ezekwe are two people of a feather. They are more than excited to behold this day. Apart from Ezekwe, Sam, no matter what he thinks I did to him, should have pretended at my funeral because of what I did for him. Where was Ezekwe when Sam had a ghastly accident in Enugu? It was I who bore the financial cost of the three surgeries he underwent in the Enugu State Teaching Hospital.

(Pauses, looks up and continues.)

Well, my only solace is in the knowledge that death awaits everyone. It may not be immediate, but it is imminent. Those who mock the dead should continue doing so. We are all bound for six-feet beneath the ground.

ACT VIII

Two Umuokpu women hold OBIANUJU, seated on the floor, as a woman shaves her head. The other Umuokpu women clap and chant a traditional song.

PROFESSOR NWOKEKE

What in God's name are you people doing to my wife's hair? This shouldn't be what I am thinking. Will you stop this obnoxious act? This is my wife. Must her hair be cut for the world to know that she is mourning? You people know how I fought this harmful traditional practise and warned that my wife should never subscribe to it.

(Attempts to collect the razor blade from the Umuokpu shaving OBIANUJU's head, but doesn't succeed.)

Oh my goodness! This must not happen. Never ever! I must call the attention of the Umunna to this!

(He hurries over to another part of the stage where the Umunna are gathered, trying to placate a furious UDENTA.)

PROFESSOR NWOKEKE

(Looks questioningly at the Umunna)

Why are you pleading with UDENTA to be calm? What on earth does a brother have to do for his sibling that I haven't done for him? I know what I did for him to further his education, but to no avail. He was the one who said he wanted to venture into business. I didn't object. I opened the business of his choice with over a million naira. Oh! That's when naira had value.

(Clears his throat).

After two years, he squandered the money on womanising and alcohol. He ran back to me like a prodigal son. Did I reject him? No! I took him back and asked him to tell me the kind of business he would like to do again. This time, he said that he wanted a 14-seater Mitsubishi bus for interstate transportation. Did I object? No! I bought the bus for him, only for him to come back six months later to tell me that the bus had been stolen. My further secret investigation into the matter shocked me to my core: Udenta sold the bus for a pittance and gave the proceeds to a lady who asked him to prove his love for her! What a dunderhead of a brother I have!

(He moves to the eldest among the Umunna.)

Ask UDENTA, who now is lamenting bitterly, what he did with the huge amount of money I gave him before your presence, after he was deported from South Africa where I sent him to better his life. I will never forget that early morning when he came with you to my house to beg and asked me to settle him for the last time. Remind him of the undertaking he signed before I wired the two million naira to his account. If I still remember, he signed that he would never disturb me again. So, why is he annoyed that I didn't include him in my will? Did I labour for him or for my children? Am I his father? He should go and disturb Chief Njoku in his grave and not me or my children. Let him not allow me to expose him before the Umunna how he connived with Ogbuokiri to extort my children in the name of making a coffin for my burial. They collected four hundred thousand naira for the coffin that was supposed to cost two hundred thousand naira. What of the catering company and the Highlife music entertainers? He doctored the receipts given to him by them and pocketed the gains without the notice of my children and wife. Since he is taking it as his right that I would have included him in my will, I would instruct EBUKA, my son, not to give him the money I asked him to compensate him with. Balderdash!

(Hisses).

Don't think I will be here listening to this gibberish coming out of his mouth.

(He walks out of the place angrily and returns to the Umuokpu. This time, his children, EBUKA and NNEOMA, are standing before Umuokpu. EBUKA is addressing the Umuokpu. Professor Nwokeke pays attention.)

EBUKA
I want to specially thank you on behalf of our family for coming out en masse to mourn the demise of my father, Professor Nwokeke.

(Pointing the two goats and tubers of yam on the ground.)

These two goats and tubers of yam are for you.
Thank you so much

PROFESSOR NWOKEKE

(Interrupts EBUKA.)

No! No! No! This is not going to happen. It is against my wish that Umuokpu leaves this house with goats and yams.

(Moves over to EBUKA.)

Ebuka, you have never in your life disobeyed me. So, take back the goats and yams. These people are nothing but gluttons! If I calculate how much food they have consumed since they came here last night, it would feed one child all through primary school.

(Frustrated that EBUKA isn't hearing him, he quickly moves over to NNEOMA.)

Ada m ji eje mba, I know you would not allow this to happen. Take back those items from them immediately.

(As he is struggling to convince his children, Umuokpu are chanting traditional songs as if they won the lottery. Professor Nwokeke fumes.)

If not for death, all these reprobate minds wouldn't have gathered here today.

Death! Oh! Death!

You can turn a lion into a dog.

You can make a king walk bare-footed while servants ride on horses.

How I wish I could overcome death!

I would have made you powerless.

I would have kept you bound where no one would ever come to save you.

(He goes to sit on his grave.)

What is the essence of throwing funeral parties?

A funeral party where money is wasted!

A funeral party where one's defeated enemies have an opportunity to spit on him!

A funeral party that allows money-mongers in the extended family to milk the deceased family dry!

A funeral party where ungrateful gluttons, gossips, and thieves and mad people congregate to live out their depravity!

A funeral party where people who didn't celebrate the deceased when he/she was alive would attend wearing colourful asoebi!

Most of the families of the deceased go into huge debts as a result of borrowing money to organise befitting funeral parties in order to feel like they belong in society!

Everyone returns to his or her home, and everything about the dead is forgotten in the twinkle of an eye!

Is a funeral party the best way to mourn the dead?

There are better ways to mourn the dead than throw big funeral parties.

Why don't you immortalise your loved one by coming up with ideas or projects that will keep him/her memory alive for ages?

Funeral parties have harmed the family of the deceased more than they have benefited, therefore if I had the power in my next life, I would outlaw them. And I mean it!

END

ACKNOWLEDGEMENTS

I thank everyone, who supported me while I worked on this project: Sunday Arekam, Odega Shawa, Ikenna Okeh, Ever Obi and Oluwatoba James Abu.

Big thanks to Nonso Efughi, for finding it worthy to create it into audio.

I am grateful to my editor at Abibiman Publishing, Ifeanyi Mojekwu and Stephen Embleton's design and to Achulike Anwuacha, who did the illustration on the book cover.

Here is a play I have always wanted to put out for a long time, until my father died.

Thanks to everyone.

Onyeka Nwelue
Oxford, 2023

www.ingramcontent.com/pod-product-compliance
Lightning Source LLC
Chambersburg PA
CBHW030311100526
44590CB00012B/590